I Love The Hell
Out Of...

I Love The Hell Out Of...

Tamera Stewart

I LOVE THE HELL OUT OF...

Scripture quotations marked NLT are taken from the Holy Bible, New Living Translation, copyright © 1996, 2004, 2007. Used by permission of Tyndale House Publishers, Inc. Carol Stream, Illinois 60188. All rights reserved. Website

Scripture quotations marked MSG are taken from THE MESSAGE. Copyright © 1993, 1994, 1995, 1996, 2000, 2001, 2002, 2003 by Eugene H. Peterson. Used by permission of NavPress Publishing Group. Website.

iUniverse books may be ordered through booksellers or by contacting:

iUniverse
1663 Liberty Drive
Bloomington, IN 47403
www.iuniverse.com
844-349-9409

Because of the dynamic nature of the Internet, any web addresses or links contained in this book may have changed since publication and may no longer be valid. The views expressed in this work are solely those of the author and do not necessarily reflect the views of the publisher, and the publisher hereby disclaims any responsibility for them.

Any people depicted in stock imagery provided by Getty Images are models, and such images are being used for illustrative purposes only.
Certain stock imagery © Getty Images.

ISBN: 978-1-6632-1021-0 (sc)
ISBN: 978-1-6632-1022-7 (e)

Library of Congress Control Number: 2020919087

Print information available on the last page.

iUniverse rev. date: 10/05/2020

Foreword

I was glad when I heard that Tamera Stewart was conquering and explaining what many deal with day after day. What people search a lifetime to understand, feel, demonstrate and have love!

Love is a powerful tool. It can up lift the brokenhearted and yet, kill the deepest dream without its presence. God intended love to carry us through hardship and joy. It was to be celebrated and honor when times were good and bad. It was designed to uplift us and chastise us. He gave his son to a people that would love him and yet crucify him.

1 Peter 4:8 states "above all, love each other deeply, because love covers a multitude of sin". So, what does that mean? To rise up from the ashes and walk in the true gift of love, we have to love the very ones that hurt us. We have to love that abusive parent, that rapist, that murder, not for the sake of them, but for your heart to be whole. Love is funny like that, one would think God has a sense a humor. Why would you require me to love the person that caused me harm? It's simple, because it heals you, and through your healing Purpose is fulfilled.

Jesus's purpose couldn't be fulfilled if HE didn't love us enough to go on the cross. Think about it, his crucifixion was love coming to save us. So, allow this book to push you to love and glean from her benefits within.

Prophetess Vatrice Davis

Introduction

I Love You, or Do I?

Love is patient and kind. Love is not jealous or boastful or proud or rude. It does not demand its own way. It is not irritable, and it keeps no record of being wronged. It does not rejoice about injustice but rejoices whenever the truth wins out. Love never gives up, never loses faith, is always hopeful, and endures through every circumstance.
—1 Corinthians 13:4–7 (NLT)

"I love you." Nothing is more powerful than those three words. Every day we say those words to someone, whether it's our spouses, our children, or a loved one. We say it. But the most important question is, Do we mean it? Are we just saying those words because we have been taught to say them? It has become almost cliché to speak the words without really knowing why you say them. First Corinthians 13 tells us that love is patient and kind. It is not rude and does not demand its own way. Well that's easier said than done. I mean, let's be honest and keep it real. We find it easy to love someone who is "easy to love." But how can we possibly love a "difficult" person?

Why should we even bother with a person who is rude or obnoxious? Simple answer: Because God loves us. I know what you're thinking, *Yeah, Tamera, I've heard it before. God gave his Son, Jesus, to the world.* And I would say, "You are correct." He did just that. What a wonderful gift Jesus is. But look at what God did. He *gave.* God gave his dear Son, his pride and joy to a world that he knew would accept and reject his gift.

Some of us would have no problem giving gifts of love to an accepting soul. But the one who would reject our gifts? I think we would be hurt, upset, mad, angry, ticked off—yes, all of that and then some. We would feel offended that we did something out of love for that person to have him or her throw it back in our faces. God knew this would happen, but he gave anyway. Great news for us. We too must give love even if it's rejected.

Oh yes. We have to love that difficult family member, rude coworker, neighbor, and enemy. We have to love that single mother who is raising children on her own and that farmer in the Midwest worried about his next harvest. We have to love that difficult boss or irritating church member. Oh yes we do. We have to love those in government or law enforcement. It is necessary. It is possible. Jesus gave us the commandment: "This is my commandment, that you love one another as I have loved you" (John 15:12 NLT).

If anyone can teach us about love and how to love it's Jesus. Think about the twelve men he selected to start his ministry. I mean, come on. They weren't an easy group to deal with. But he loved them. Let's take a look at Matthew

4:18. Jesus meets Simon, also called Peter, and Andrew. He also meets James and his brother, John. But look at what Jesus did.

> Jesus called out to them, "Come, follow me and I will show you how to fish for people." And they left their nets at once and followed him. (Matthew 4:19–20 NLT)

These men were fishermen. They made their living going out on boats and catching whatever went inside their nets. Jesus came to them and told them to follow him. Wait. Hold on a minute. Are you kidding me? Did they give up their incomes and occupations to follow Jesus? Yes, they did. Did you see what happened here? They walked away from it all to learn from Jesus.

That is love.

They were going to go out and fish for souls or bring souls to Christ.

That is love.

It would take an enormous amount of love for anyone to walk away from his or her job. And then on top of that, notice that Jesus never mentioned to them anything about replacing their incomes or getting paid. Loving someone requires you to give up a familiar comfort. I'm not saying to walk away from your job into full-time ministry, unless God has called you into that. No, what I am saying is that when you love Christ and follow his commands, you don't need to worry about anything. The disciples gave up that comfort of income and followed. We can do the same.

Remember our opening scripture in 1 Corinthians 13? Love never gives up, never loses faith; it is always hopeful. Please understand, my friend. You have to come to a point in life where you drop your net, follow Christ, and love on people. Don't give up on people; don't lose faith in God. Of course life would be a breeze if people were easy to love. But it won't always be like that. I pray as you read this book you will get a better understanding of how to love people even when they are difficult to love. I pray that you will see how loving on people is pleasing to God.

But the one thing I want you to see is that even though Jesus is our perfect Savior, his church is not so perfect. We will learn about a church that had a leader who was not so loving, yet other followers of Christ did love. Isn't the church a place of love? It should be. But not everyone in the church walked in love. Our response will be that of love. Glory to God.

Exercise

Before we go any further, let's do a few exercises. Think about a person or people you have a hard time showing love to. Be honest; this is between God and you. Get a notebook or journal. Make it your "Love Book." Take a sheet of paper, and fold it in half. On one side, write down the names of these people. On the other side, write a brief description of what they have done or said to make you feel that way. How are they hard to love? Keep your journal at hand. At the end I will share some scriptures to help with showing love toward other people, plus a direct prophetic page the Lord has shared with me.

Prayer

Heavenly Father, I thank you for the people reading this book. God, thank you for showing us all how to walk in love. Thank you for first loving us by giving us the gift of your Son, Jesus. Bring the words and pages to life as they read. Speak to the readers this very hour. You are worthy, in Jesus's name. Amen.

Chapter 1

I Love Trouble(makers)

So now I am giving you a new commandment: Love
each other. Just as I have loved you, you should
love each other. Your love for one another will
prove to the world that you are my disciples.
—John 13:34–35 (NLT)

There was a popular song written back in 1965 by Jackie
DeShannon called "What the World Needs Now." Over
the years, it was rerecorded by other artists who put their
own flairs to it. But the first verse of the song stood out, the
lyrics almost prophetic.

> What the world needs now is love sweet
> love It's the only thing that there's just too
> little of What the world needs now is love
> sweet love. No not just for some but for
> everyone.

1

If there was a time when we needed more love, it would be now. With so much going on in this world, it's almost hard to feel or see the love. But not just any love, sweet love. A little extra. We see our government officials, senators, pastors, family members—all those we are surrounded by—but no one seems to show the love that Christ was speaking of. I can understand how hard that is to grasp. How is it possible that people who speak of God show no love?

Trust me, I have had my personal struggles. I was one of those people who did not know how to love in spite of. I would wear my feelings on my sleeves and avoid all contact with people. But I thank God for growth. I thank God for understanding. In the scripture above, Jesus is telling us how to have love for others and prove to the world who we are in him. He never commanded us to only love the easy people. If that were the case, we may only love one person—and that's stretching it. God wants us to love everyone. And yes, there are some difficult souls to love. They are everywhere.

You probably know a few of them, people who are always causing problems. They never want to see you or anyone else prosper or grow. They try to block everything and anything, usually with little success. Who are these people? You guessed it, troublemakers.

We all know one or two. Okay, maybe three. You might even be one. What exactly is a troublemaker? You just can't walk up to a person and decide, *I think he's a troublemaker.* What are troublemakers' motives? What should you do about them? *Merriam-Webster's Dictionary* defines a troublemaker as a person who consciously or unconsciously causes troubles. Oh, please, that doesn't help. In other words, they are aware or not aware of their actions. To put it simply, some do not cause trouble on purpose, and others get pleasure from causing trouble.

Is it possible to love such people? They cause trouble on purpose. They make it their job to tell lies or speak hate. Yes, it is possible. And necessary.

Jesus said in Luke 6:27–28 (NLT), "But to you who are willing to listen, I say; love your enemies! Do good to those who hate you. Bless those who curse you. Pray for those who hurt you." Jesus knew some people would reject this, because he starts off by saying, "who are willing to listen." He knew some wouldn't like to hear the next part: "love your enemies." Jesus was not asking us to be doormats and just let them walk over us. Of course not. He was saying to love them in their nasty attitudes and bad tempers, because he loves them with their nasty attitudes and bad tempers. This is pleasing to God.

In all honesty, it's not even about other people. They try to make it about themselves by the way they treat you or speak to you. But don't make it about them. Don't consume yourself with worry about how they feel. Leave that to God. No, just love them and pray for them. Yes, you can love the hell right out of people. Yes, you can love trouble. I don't mean trouble in the sense of chaos and confusion but the hell that is inside that person. I don't know about you, but sometimes if a person I meet is being difficult or spiteful, I laugh. Not so much at that person but at the fact that I can recognize what it is. I recognize that this might just be a test I have to pass. And we just love taking a test, right? Well, maybe not. But it is necessary to pass it.

Let us think of a scenario that could be possible. You, your spouse, and children live on five acres of land. Say this is family land that has been passed down from generation to generation. It is rural, far from the nearest city, and there are only dirt roads. Now if you know anything about rural living, you know there are plenty of dirt roads. One of the roads is really bad. I mean it's bumpy, has deep holes, and is uneven. If it rains, forget it. You aren't able to even drive on it.

Now there is another dirt road that is much better. It's a little uneven, but not that bad. Imagine you are surrounded by other family members. Everyone uses the "good road," but certain family members won't allow you to use that road unless you pay them to use it. Oh yes. They want you to pay them to use it. If you don't pay them, they call the police on you and even threaten to shoot you and your family. All of this comes from hate and spite. How do you respond?

Take it easy, my friend. I know you probably had a flashback about people treating you wrong. You remember all the hate they gave. Yes, those troublemakers.

But what if I told you it's not about them? What if I told you that the hell in them is easier to love than you realize? Read John 13:34–35 and Romans 13:8. Instead of giving the same hate, respond with love. There will be those who say you are justified in responding like them. They will almost mock you for not hating them back.

The one thing Jesus did not do was respond negatively to doubters. And he still doesn't. He did the opposite. He gave love even while correcting them. Doesn't he do that for us today? I could write another book on all the things I have done wrong, and Jesus met me with love. Our stories continue.

We must constantly show love to people every day. Jesus never said that loving people would be easy. If it were, Satan wouldn't stand a chance. Remember our opening scripture, 1 Corinthians 13:4–7. It says love is patient and kind, but not easy.

We can do it, my friend. We can love like Christ. He gives us the strength (Philippians 4:13). Don't respond like the troublemakers. Love the hell out of them. Praise God.

But They Are Being So Difficult

One thing we must understand about people who are difficult to love is that they really don't understand the power of God's love for them. I mean, people can say, "I love God," or, "I love other people," but do their actions align with their words? Earlier we saw how some of the disciples gave up their incomes to follow Jesus and become "lovers of men and women." Why did they do that? Because they knew the love Jesus gave them, and they loved him back. So they wanted to share that same love. They wanted other people to experience the same love.

We can love the hell out of people. Yes we can. The world needs to see it. People need to feel it. Pray for them. Be kind to them. Love them. God will handle the rest.

"But they are being so difficult!" I know they are, and it's frustrating. Sometimes we never know why some people are difficult to love. There might just be some underlying hurt inside them. Not everyone knows how to handle stress or rejection. To some, the people who should have loved them hurt them. We just don't know. But God knows. He knows all about it.

Our commandment is to love. Love is patient. Love is kind. And we can show the world what true love is, my friend. Oh yes, we can love the troublemaker. As the song says, "Trouble don't last always." Stand firm on the Word. Keep loving people. Keep loving. We are Jesus's disciples. "What the world needs now is love sweet love." To God be the glory.

Chapter 2

I Love the Truth

When Jesus started his ministry, he selected twelve men who became his disciples. These men followed him, studied under him, and sat at his feet. They learned in depth from Jesus, which I am sure was both exciting and confusing.

There was one disciple who was fascinated me. That was John. What was it about him that was intriguing? For one thing, Jesus called him and his brother, James, "sons of thunder" (Mark 3:17). There was something about John that made Jesus give him a nickname.

My nickname is Tammy. I've been known by that name for as long as I can remember. Not too many people know my real name is Tamera, even some family members. I am not particularly fond of that name, but there's no need to complain now. Maybe I look like a Tammy. Or act like a Tammy. I don't know. Whatever the reason, that is the name I am known by.

Jesus gave John the nickname "Thunder." What would make Jesus do this? He could have just called him Jay or something simple, but he used Thunder. Think about this. When a rainstorm comes, it's usually accompanied by thunder and lightning. Thunder is loud, noisy, and frightening. If you listen long enough, it almost sounds angry. It's not a pleasant sound. John had a characteristic that Jesus was trying to point out to him. John, along with his brother, was probably loud, noisy, and a little frightening. It would be rather difficult to learn from Jesus if you are always loud. And to love someone with anger would defeat the purpose. How can you love if you are always angry? It's impossible. Look back at 1 Corinthians 13:4–7. It says love is not irritable. Don't get frustrated. Love on people and lose the irritation. God continues to love on us daily despite our faults.

So Jesus was pointing out the type of person John was. His nickname said it all. I wouldn't want a nickname like that.

A loving thing about Jesus is that he selected John despite knowing how he acted. Now it was time to teach him a new way, a new commandment, a better way to respond. But don't be hard on poor John. He was just like most of us. I'm almost certain he spoke before thinking and didn't bite his tongue. He had his good moments and bad ones, good days and bad days. Don't we get like that sometimes? We are not perfect, so don't try to be. Just allow Jesus to teach you. He will show us how to love more. Praise God.

He (Jesus) Came for Everyone

So far we know that John had a few issues. Not only was he known by his nickname but he was a bit of a troublemaker as well. Oh yes, he had his moments. The disciples grew closer and closer to Jesus. I think they got it in their minds that Jesus was exclusively for them and only them. But John quickly learned how Jesus felt about troublemakers.

Jesus and his disciples had arrived in Capernaum, the small village where some of the disciples were from. In Mark 9:38–42, we learn about a person in the village who was using Jesus's name to cast out demons. The scripture doesn't say whether this was a man or woman. This person was most likely one of those in the crowd that saw the miracles of Jesus. This person was probably told his or her whole life that he or she wasn't worthy of the love of God. The sad thing is the person believed it—until Jesus came. The other disciples didn't give their opinions, but John, for some reason or another, took issue with this.

John said to Jesus, "Teacher, we saw someone using your name to cast out demons, but we told him to stop because he wasn't in our group" (Mark 9:38 NLT). Notice what John said here: "our group," meaning that because we walk with Christ, hang out with him, and learn directly from him, "others" are not welcome. In John's mind, only the inner circle could feel the love of Christ. I think it's fair to say that John was a troublemaker. He tried to keep someone from Jesus. But how I love my Savior. Look at how Jesus responded:

> "Don't stop him!" Jesus said. "No one who performs a miracle in my name will soon be able to speak evil of me. Anyone who is not against us is for us. If anyone gives you even a cup of water because you belong to the Messiah, I tell you the truth, that

person will surely be rewarded. But if you cause one of these little ones who trusts in me to fall into sin, it would be better for you to be thrown into the sea with a large millstone hung around your neck." (Mark 9:39–42 NLT)

I like how the Message Bible breaks it down.

Jesus wasn't pleased. "Don't stop him. No one can use my name to do something good and powerful, and in the next breath cut me down. If he's not an enemy, he's an ally. Why, anyone by just giving you a cup of water in my name is on our side. Count on it that God will notice. On the other hand, if you give one of these simple, childlike believers a hard time, bullying or taking advantage of their simple trust, you'll soon wish you hadn't. You'd be better off dropped in the middle of the lake with a millstone around your neck." (Mark 9:39–42 MSG)

My goodness. Jesus shut John down quick. He had to reiterate to John and the other disciples what the mission was. It wasn't about a selected few or the good ol' boys club. No, it's a love thing. What's love got to do with it? Everything. The truth is Jesus showed them that if people are real in their love for him, then they won't be able to speak in his name and then curse his name in the same breath.

But you know what we sometimes do? We feel like this person is not worthy of speaking in Jesus's name. Jesus never mentioned the person's salvation, faith, or beliefs. This man or woman in the village may have been excluded all of his or her life. Keep in mind the type of leadership that was present in those days. Bondage was real. Jesus's love for them brought on confidence. It brought on hope, change, and most importantly, love.

Love on that individual the same way. You will know if this person has real love for Christ and people just by the way the individual speaks or carries his- or herself. Trust me when I say God doesn't need our help. We don't need to go through someone's spiritual résumé to check qualifications. Just love and then love some more. We can do it, my friend.

Let's look at a similar incident that happened with Moses in Numbers 11:26–30 (NLT).

> Two men, Eldad and Medad, had stayed behind in the camp. They were listed among the elders, but they had not gone out to the Tabernacle. Yet the Spirit rested upon them as well, so they prophesied there in the camp. A young man ran and reported to Moses, "Eldad and Medad are prophesying in the camp!"
>
> Joshua son of Nun, who had been Moses' assistant since his youth, protested, "Moses, my master, make them stop!" But Moses replied, "Are you jealous for my sake? I wish that all the Lord's people were prophets and

11

that the Lord would put his Spirit upon
them all!" Then Moses returned to the
camp with the elders of Israel.

During this incident, the children of Israel were complaining to Moses about almost everything, from not having enough food (then God provided more than enough food) to hardships. Whatever it was, they complained. Eldad and Medad were prophesying to the people. The Spirit of God rested upon them, so they told the people what God told them. They were speaking for God, not themselves. The only problem was that they did not go to the tabernacle. Oh my goodness! That means they didn't go to church, if we were using modern-day terms. They didn't go into God's dwelling place to pray. But keep in mind, the Spirit was still on them.

A young man ran to tell Moses what happened, and Joshua took exception to this. He wanted Moses to stop them from prophesying to the people. Joshua felt they didn't fit the mold; they were just average people. But Moses told Joshua the same thing Jesus told John: Don't you dare stop people from loving other people. Joshua and John weren't looking at the situation with love. That is how some people, especially church folks, are today. They disqualify other people because they may not go to the same church or have the same denomination.

Trust me when I say my thinking was like that of Joshua and John. I felt certain people didn't belong. I looked down on them until God got a hold of me. I soon found myself feeling like the very ones I had condemned. I have never called myself a prophet, but I know that I walk in the prophetic. See, right now some people just rolled their eyes after reading that. I smile at that. My friend, please be careful of how you disqualify other people. Stop worrying about whether they believe in Christ. God can use whomever he chooses to do his work.

Our job is to love on those people. Talk to God about how you feel. I had to do that. They may not have the same passion or fire that you have, but God can still use them. The more you love, the more it shows them God's love. Continue to share the love of God. To all my church folks, please seek God about how you feel. I have witnessed many people in the church run others out. You got it in your mind that certain people were not qualified, so they had to go. You didn't preach the truth to start with, so now you are upset because God is using them. Shame on you. Jesus already said that people couldn't bless in his name and curse his name in the same breath. If they are not with Jesus, then they are against him. Evil is in them, and God will deal with that. Don't stop loving, my dear. Don't stop. Jesus came here to love on people. He came so the oppressed would be set free (Luke 4:18), so sinners would be called to repent (Mark 2:17), to do the will of the Father (John 6:38), and to live in the truth (John 8:31–32).

Okay, Jesus, I'm Ready to Love

Now it was time for Jesus to leave the earth physically. The disciples had three years of hands-on education, so it was time to start. Time to love on John. As Jesus was on the cross, some of his family and friends were there. John; Jesus's mother, Mary; and Mary Magdalene were forced to watch in horror at this wonderful gift—giving up his life in love for the world. But even in his final moments, Jesus gave one last lesson on love to John. This time his mother, Mary, would be part of it.

Look at John 19:26–27 (NLT). "When Jesus saw his mother standing beside the disciple he loved, he said to her, 'Dear woman, here is your son.' And he said to this disciple, 'Here is your mother.' And from then on, this disciple took her into his home."

Now think about this. In the natural, Mary is the biological/birth mother of Jesus. She carried him inside her body until it was time to deliver. She loved him, nursed him, and provided for him. He was her baby. She was there when he took his first steps. She taught him to speak, to eat, and to read. She was his mother. That is what God called her to be.

But now Jesus had to show his mother it was time for her to become John's "mother." What do I mean by that? Well, we already know what a mother does in the natural. Let's now flip it and look at the spiritual. Jesus taught John about loving on people. I'm pretty sure his mother learned as well. But what Jesus was telling them, and us as well, was that Mary would now be the spiritual leader that John needed in his ministry. Oh yes. John's ministry was beginning. He was ready. And so are we.

It was time for John to go out and spread the gospel, the love of Christ, and the love of God to the world. Mary was his covering. And what exactly is a covering? A covering is something that covers, conceals, protects, or surrounds. Jesus's birth mother would now become John's spiritual mother. She would cover him and protect him. She would correct him when he was wrong and make sure he was speaking truth, speaking God's Word. All this would be done in love. If you ever become a covering over someone's life, or maybe you already are, you must remember to speak the truth to that individual. Or you may have a covering, a spiritual leader over your life. Listen to that person as he or she is feeding you. This will help you build strength, build endurance. This will show you and me how to love more, as this covering is led by the Holy Spirit. It's a wonderful thing. Praise God for the covering.

So now we see how Mary became the spiritual mother to John. We see how his ministry began that very day. But take a look at the next part of this scripture. The last part is significant: "And from then on, this disciple took her into his home." In the natural, Mary moved into John's home. She would live with him and be his mother. But think about it in the spirit. A home is a place of comfort, a haven. Notice it didn't say he took her into his house. When you look at a house, it is a building. Yes, we all live in houses, but home is where the heart is. A house can be destroyed, demolished, or torn down.

Remember the movie *The Wizard of Oz*? Dorothy kept saying, "There's no place like home, there's no place like home." To her, that home was a place of love. It was a safe place. It was warm and kind and filled with love. John opened his home, his heart, to Mary. Friends, make sure that you open your home, your heart, to people. Love on them. Our homes could be our jobs or our churches. So many people go to work or church each day and feel no love. The atmosphere is dull and downright uncomfortable. You never know what that person may need for that day. He or she may just need a smile. So open your home, your heart. You can show that person how to love the hell out of whatever it is. Praise God.

I pray that you have developed an understanding of how loving people is important to God. We saw how Jesus taught the disciples, especially John, the importance of this truth. So now let's see what John learned. How did he handle this thing called love?

Let the Loving Begin

Let's take an in-depth look at 3 John. We will study the letters that John wrote to the church and certain leaders in the church. We will see how some leaders responded in love and some did not. Oh yes. There was trouble in the church back then just as there is now. What did John say in those letters? Who was the leader who loved? Who was the leader who did not love? How did the church respond?

Allow the Holy Spirit to speak to you as you study these pages. Let him guide you. Maybe you have had enough of church and the people in the church. That is fine. Jesus knows exactly what you are going through. See how others dealt with those issues. See how they loved the hell out of people. Let us pray:

Heavenly Father, thank you for the gift of love. I confess to you now that I have not always shown love to people in my actions and my words. I ask for your forgiveness. I thank you for loving me even when I didn't show love to you. I declare and decree that from this day on, I will walk in love. I may not always agree with people, but I will love them anyway. Here is my heart, Lord. I surrender all to you. In Jesus's name. Amen.

Chapter 3

I Love the Truth

This letter is from John, the elder. I am writing to Gaius, my dear friend, whom I love in the truth. Dear friend, I hope all is well with you and that you are as healthy in body as you are strong in spirit. Some of the traveling teachers recently returned and made me very happy by telling me about your faithfulness and that you are living according to the truth. I could have no greater joy than to hear that my children are following the truth.
—3 John 1–4 (NLT)

The elder unto the well-beloved Gaius, whom I love in the truth. Beloved, I wish above all things that thou mayest prosper and be in health, even as thy soul prospereth. For I rejoiced greatly, when the brethren came and testified of the truth that is in thee, even as thou walkest in the truth. I have no greater joy than to hear that my children walk in truth.
—3 John 1–4 (KJV)

I remember a few years back I was so sick I could barely walk or talk. I'm not sure if I had the flu, but I was in pretty bad shape. I had no appetite whatsoever and really didn't want to be bothered with people. I was in no mood to deal with anyone's drama, let alone help them in anyway. I know that I complained about being sick and was upset and moody. I was just not a nice person at that time. I let my physical condition keep me down and made sure everyone knew about it. I mean, let's be real. I had every right to cut people off. I was sick. My body was not well. Didn't I deserve to feel the way I felt? Or did I? In the opening of 3 John, we read the letter that John wrote to Gaius. Not much is known about Gaius, but we do know that he was beloved by John and something was wrong with his health.

A sickness or illness is unhealthy to the body or mind. It could cause some physical ailments or physical deformity. It has a tendency to stop us in our tracks, making it impossible to be of use to anyone. It could cause weakness, and therefore, we lose strength. But look at what John said to Gaius in verse 2: "Dear friend, I hope all is well with you and that you are as healthy in body as you are strong in spirit." John doesn't say how he heard about Gaius's poor health. Being that they are friends, I'm almost convinced he saw Gaius from time to time and knew he was sick. But it was something that John witnessed from Gaius's attitude or demeanor that caused him not to dwell on his sickness. Gaius could have easily thought, *Well look, I am sick. I don't feel well, so I can't pray today. I can't spend time in God's Word. I don't feel like dealing with difficult people today.* And he would have been right.

But let's study the second part of that scripture: "I hope all is well with you and that you are as healthy in body as you are strong in spirit." Gaius was strong in his spirit. Hold on a minute. How could this man be strong in spirit but weak in his body? Well, let's see how another great man of God dealt with this. Let's read 2 Corinthians 12:1–10.

My Pain, His Glory

In 2 Corinthians 12:1–10, we read a portion of the letter that the apostle Paul wrote to the church in Corinth. In it, he spoke of the visions and revelations he had from God. It dealt with his out-of-body experience and how he was in heaven. Paul could have boasted about this experience, giving himself all the credit. But he didn't.

> If I wanted to boast, I would be no fool in doing so, because I would be telling the truth. But I won't do it, because I don't want anyone to give me credit beyond what they can see in my life or hear in my message, even though I have received such wonderful revelations from God. So to keep me from becoming proud, I was given a thorn in my flesh, a messenger from Satan to torment me and keep me from becoming proud. (2 Corinthians 12:6–7NLT)

Great job, Paul! You did not take credit for something you had no control over. You are free and clear of any problems or discomforts in your life. You are a man of God, and a Christian doesn't have to go through tough times. You gave all credit and praise to God for what you have done. But it wasn't so, my friend. Paul was given a "thorn" in his flesh. There has always been this misconception that Christians are immune to hardship. That once we are saved and give our lives to Jesus, *poof!* No more problems. But that is not so.

Merriam-Webster's Dictionary describes a thorn as something that causes distress or irritation. Well good Lord, that could be just about anything. The Bible doesn't give a clear indication what that thorn was in Paul's flesh, but one thing is certain: It wasn't comfortable. How could this be? Why would God allow Paul to receive this thorn if he did nothing wrong? Let's continue.

> Three different times I begged the Lord to take it away. Each time he said, "My grace is all you need. My power works best in weakness." So now I am glad to boast about my weaknesses, so that the power of Christ can work through me. That's why I take pleasure in my weaknesses, and in the insults, hardships, persecutions, and troubles that I suffer for Christ. For when I am weak, then I am strong. (2 Corinthians 12:8–10 NLT)

Paul must have lost his mind. I mean, did he just welcome these thorns that caused him so much grief? Yes, he did. But it wasn't so much that he was enjoying the pain. No one enjoys being in pain. It hurts. We want it to go away. No, Paul was stating how, in his weakness, the power of Christ worked best through him. God was using Paul as an example to show others how to depend on him for everything they have and how to love God unconditionally.

Instead of Paul complaining about the pain, he continued to spread the love of Christ to others. People were watching. They knew something was wrong with Paul, but he continued to show love toward them. While in his pain, God received all the glory, all the praise. My God! What a mighty God we serve. God's grace was enough for Paul. It was enough to get him through his afflictions. And this takes us back to Gaius. Gaius was strong in his spirit. God's grace was enough for him. Though his body was weak, he was still strong in Christ. My friends, whatever thorn you have in your life, know that God's grace is enough. It may not feel good, and we may not always feel up to the task, but love on people. When you love on them, they see Christ through you. If they see you going through something while you continue to share the love of Christ, mighty things will happen. When we have total dependence on God, it keeps us humble. Gaius was humble, just like Paul. They never moaned or complained about those thorns. They took it, gave God credit, and continued to love. Praise God.

As we continue reading John's letter, word got back to him from the traveling teachers about Gaius. These were missionary workers who were spreading the gospel and the love of Christ. They would go from city to city, town to town. Along the way they experienced rejection and hate, but they also experienced love. Love from people that wanted to hear about Jesus. And they met Gaius. It had an obvious effect on their lives, and they made sure to share it with John: "Some of the traveling teachers recently returned and made me very happy by telling me about your faithfulness and that you are living according to the truth. I could have no greater joy than to hear that my children are following the truth" (3 John 3–4 NLT).

Notice it says, "some of the traveling teachers." It does not give a specific number, but I think we can conclude that not everyone in the group shared with John their encounter with Gaius. Some may have fallen off along the way; some may have died. We are not sure. But we do know that some were touched by him. Gaius spoke the truth while walking in the truth. My God, this man lived according to the Word of God. He did not sugarcoat the teachings of Christ to make people feel good about their sins.

> Jesus said, "I am the way, and the truth, and the life. No one comes to the Father except through me." (John 14:5 NLT)

> For the wrath of God is revealed from Heaven against all ungodliness and unrighteousness of men, who by their unrighteousness suppresses the truth. (Romans 1:18 NLT)

And the Truth Shall

The opposite of a lie is the truth. Simply put, there is no possible way that you can tell a lie but then say it is the truth. But that is what some people do. They even suppress the truth because it's hard to accept.

I try not to watch the news that often because of the craziness in the world. Maybe I should. Lord knows there needs to be intercessory prayer. But I do remember someone got on one of the major news channels and stated that they were giving "alternative facts" about a particular situation. What? Are you serious? Alternative facts? To me that is nothing but a lie, not truth.

Think about this. Let's say someone shares with you that he or she lost $500. It was his or her rent money, gas money—but now it's gone. That would be a fact. This person has lost the money, and it's not coming back. But say you found out the truth, that the person lost the money gambling, playing the lotto. or spending it loosely. How would you feel about this person when you found out the truth?

The person made sure to tell you that he or she lost the money but didn't tell you how. You might look at the person differently if you knew. What the truth does is to convict or convince us that we are wrong. And not many people want to admit that they are wrong. It is not our job to worry about whether that person is living according to the Word of God; it is to love on that person. Yes, we are to be concerned for the person's soul. We would hate to see anyone perish. But don't worry about it. Don't consume yourself with unnecessary anxiety.

When we speak the truth and spread the gospel, we do this out of love. Our love will drive that hell right out. Love the hell out of them. Pray the hell out of them. I am not saying that we have to accept everything under the sun or be complacent about it.

My friend, let the truth *always* be in you. We will be ridiculed for standing for the truth on the Word of God. Don't let people try to convince you that the sky is red when you know it's blue. So call it what it is. Don't twist the Word of God to please people or get them to like you. Love on Jesus, stand for the truth, and watch God work.

I have heard some people say they have "evolved" on certain issues. Don't try to explain a lie. Don't try to make it come true. Just stand on the Word of God and love. We can, however, evolve in our treatment of people, change in the way we have acted. Show more love. But you can't evolve on lies. That means you agree with them. If Jesus said it wasn't true, we won't say it is. Praise God.

People Notice Us

So these traveling teachers told of Gaius living according to the truth. He was spreading the gospel in love and was faithful in doing this. John was full of joy about this. Remember that John learned by walking with Jesus. And then it was his turn to share that same love, to speak the truth. And he did that. Gaius was a student of John's. John was that covering over his life; he was a spiritual father. Remember how John had a covering over him as well. Now it was his turn.

My friend, walk in truth. People are noticing us. They are watching. They are listening. You are not judging people when you speak the truth, but they will say that you are. Love on them. Don't compromise the Word of God. Even in your weakness, even when you feel your spiritual tank running on empty, God will fill you up. His glory will shine through. We can do this. We can love the hell out of people. Praise God.

Chapter 4

I Love Giving (My Money)

Each one must give as he has decided in his heart, not
reluctantly or under compulsion, for God loves a cheerful giver.
—2 Corinthians 9:7 (NLT)

Yes, my friend, you read it correctly. The words *giving* and
money. These two words have been the most controversial
ever spoken in the church. And yet here we are again, talking
about them. Before you panic, let's think about exactly what
giving is. When we give to someone, we are transferring or
delivering something to that person. It is leaving us and
going to someone else.

All of us have given something. Whether it be our time,
our food, or our space, we have given it. But why do we have
such a hard time giving our money? There is this belief that
preachers are getting rich off the money or the giving of the
members. Meanwhile, the members are suffering without
any financial growth or harvest. Is this correct?

In some cases this may be true. There are a selected group of preachers who are superrich. Are they taking from their churches? It's hard to say. The members of those churches should hold their preachers accountable by asking to see where their money is going. But I am talking about giving in general. What about those small, local churches? What about the church in your town or community that doesn't have a super rich preacher? Why don't the members give more?

We are often more concerned about giving to humanity rather than pleasing God. We worry about what's in it for us instead of how it will please God. Take a look at 3 John 1:5–8 (NLT):

> Dear friend, you are being faithful to God when you care for the traveling teachers who pass through, even though they are strangers to you. They have told the church here of your loving friendship. Please continue providing for such teachers in a manner that pleases God. For they are traveling for the Lord, and they accept nothing from people who are not believers. So we ourselves should support them so that we can be their partners as they teach the truth.

Here we read another letter that John wrote to Gaius. Remember we already learned that Gaius was not in the best of health, but it did not stop him from spreading Christ's love. So even in his physical weakness, he was strong in spirit.

He lived according to the truth and would not compromise the Word of God. We got that.

But John wrote something interesting. In verses 5 and 6, he told Gaius that he was being faithful to God when he cared for the traveling teachers. But the kicker is, they were strangers to him. Now let's get this straight. Gaius was not in great physical shape and gave love. Now he was caring for people he didn't even know.

Yes, my friend. He did.

According to *Merriam-Webster's Dictionary*, when you care for someone or something, you have an interest or concern, a liking or fondness. Gaius cared for these traveling teachers. Remember that these were missionary workers going from town to town, spreading the gospel. I'm pretty sure they traveled from faraway and had no place to lay their heads. He had a concern for them, a fondness for them, most likely because they were both lovers of Jesus. They were both standing on the truth.

But I also believe it was because they had no place to really rest and sleep for the night. I am almost convinced that Gaius opened his home to these teachers. Can you imagine that, opening your home to strangers? We wouldn't do that for just anyone. But when you have other believers spreading the love of Christ, you will open your home and your heart to them.

Can we remember who else opened their homes? It was John, Gaius's spiritual father. John opened his home, his heart, to Mary, the mother of Jesus. This time we see Gaius doing the same. Gaius learned from John about caring for others with love. His spiritual father taught him how to show that love to other people, especially strangers. How wonderful that is!

> When God's people are in need, be ready to help them. Always be eager to practice hospitality. (Romans 12:13 NLT)

> Keep on loving each other as brothers and sisters. Don't forget to show hospitality to strangers, for some who have done this have entertained angels without realizing it. (Hebrews 13:1–2 NLT)

Not only did Gaius care for these teachers, he provided for them as well.

> They have told the church here of your loving friendship. Please continue providing for such teachers in a manner that pleases God. For they are traveling for the Lord, and they accept nothing from people who are not believers. So we ourselves should support them so that we can be their partners as they teach the truth. (3 John 6–8 NLT)

According to *Merriam-Webster's Dictionary*, the word *provide* means to supply or make available (something wanted or needed). Let's think about this. If these teachers are traveling and spreading the gospel and the love of Jesus, what is the one thing they will probably need most?

Did you guess it? I know you did. Yes, it's money. Whether we want to face it or not, a ministry needs money to spread the love of Jesus. I have heard so many people say they stopped going to church because, "All they want is my money." Well, I am here to say you are half correct. Churches do need our money to stay afloat. The lights must be paid, as well rent, taxes, and feeding the community. Whatever is attached to that ministry needs to be paid.

Now let me ask this. We all shop at grocery stores or eat in fancy restaurants. Don't you think they want our money too? Have we stopped going to those establishments? My guess would be no. There are big-time CEOs who make more money in one year than some of us will see in a lifetime. But we still give our money. We keep going back. So why is the church on people's hit list? We are not giving our money to promote someone else. When we give, it must be—it has to be—unto God. But let's dig a little deeper into what John said to Gaius. He told him to continue providing for the teachers. Hold on a minute. He must continue providing. When you continue doing something, it usually means you maintain what you were doing previously without interruption. So if Gaius is told to continue providing, this means that he has been giving his money already. This is not the first time.

My God, what a powerful revelation. He didn't stop. He didn't give up on God. He didn't stop going to church because he felt people were taking from him. No. What he did was to continue his love for people. God was surely pleased with Gaius. I know what some of you may be thinking. "But Tamera, what about those people who make more money than me. They are loaded. They don't need my money."

See, my friend, the problem is we always look at the material things a person has acquired compared to what we have. We look at preachers or pastors, those with a title, as being rich enough or wealthy enough. We think they don't need our money. But let's take it a little further. Maybe people need more from you than just money. Let's take a look at Titus 3:12–14 (NLT).

In this book, Paul wrote a letter to Titus about his leadership in overseeing and organizing the churches on the island of Crete. In these verses, Paul showed Titus how to respond to the two men he was sending his way. These two men would be taking over Titus's duties on the island.

> I am planning to send either Artemas or Tychicus to you. As soon as one of them arrives, do your best to meet me at Nicopolis, for I have decided to stay there for the winter. Do everything you can to help Zenas the lawyer and Apollos with their trip. See that they are given everything they need. Our people must learn to do good by meeting the urgent needs of others; they will not be unproductive. (Titus 3:12–15 NLT)

Paul wrote about another set of men. These two men were just like the traveling teachers that interacted with Gaius. They were traveling ministers/teachers. Apollos was an unapologetic teacher of the gospel. Read his story in Acts 18:24–26.

And then there was Zenas. Not much is known about Zenas, but the one thing we know is that he was a lawyer. Now correct me if I am wrong, but when I hear about someone being a lawyer, the first thing I think about is that they are paid. In other words, they have plenty of money. But in this text, Paul was trying to show Titus that even though Zenas was a lawyer, which put him in a higher tax bracket than others, he was still doing the work of Christ and needed to be provided for. Paul does not specifically state that these men needed money, but I think it's fair to say money helps, especially when you are spreading the gospel. Whatever capacity of ministry, money is needed. But money may not be the only thing they need.

Remember that Titus was taught by Paul. He was overseer of the churches in Crete (Titus 1:5). He was the one who organized, planned, and showed the leaders of the church how to lead. So it's fair to say that Titus was a leader. He had organizational skills and could most likely handle pressure. Now here comes these two men, one being a lawyer who most likely had no leadership skills. Titus had to train them as well. They not only needed money to spread the gospel, they needed training. Can you imagine them out there on an island (literally) with no clue as to which end was up?

You, my friend, have an important role in ministry. Whatever it is that God has called you to do, do it to please him. Don't think that the church just wants your money, though that is important. You may have a gift or talent that is needed to enhance God's kingdom. You may encounter someone in ministry who could learn under you. He or she needs what you have.

Think about what happened with Gaius and Titus. Both men provided for these teachers, these ministers. Whether it was money, their time, their home, or their gifts, it was given to them. It was all done in love. And God was pleased with them. Praise God.

Chapter 5

The Loveless Leader
(Love in Spite of Them)

I wrote to the church about this, but Diotrephes, who loves
to be the leader, refuses to have anything to do with us.
When I come, I will report some of the things he is doing
and the evil accusations he is making against us. Not only
does he refuse to welcome the traveling teachers, he also
tells others not to help them. And when they do help, he
puts them out of the church. Dear friend, don't let this bad
example influence you. Follow only what is good. Remember
those who do good prove that they are God's children, and
those who do evil prove that they do not know God.
—3 John 9–11 (NLT)

I wrote unto the church; but Diotrephes, who loveth to have
the preeminence among them, receiveth us not. Wherefore,
if I come, I will remember his deeds which he doeth, praying
against us with malicious words; and not content therewith,
neither doth he himself receive the brethren, and forbiddeth
them that would, and casteth them out of the church. Beloved,

follow not that which is evil, but that which is good. He that doeth good is of God; but he that doeth evil hath not seen God.
—3 John 9–11 (KJV)

The Devil Made Me Do It

Back in 1994, there was a popular faith-based television show called *Touched by an Angel*. It starred Della Reese and Roma Downey. It was a very popular show among Christians (it was one of my favorites). In this show the actors portrayed angels. They were sent by God to come to earth to help people deal with life and things that were stopping them from prospering.

One of my favorite episodes was "Breaking Bread." It was about a small town that had to deal with some evil events that occurred. A man named Matt owned a bakery in town. One night as he was closing up the bakery, two white supremacists attacked his black assistant. Matt witnessed the whole thing but would not come forth to speak about it because of he was afraid. The two young men came to the bakery the next day to find out if Matt knew anything. The two men started to get loud with Monica (one of the angels), when a young mechanic named Derek came into the bakery. Derek confronted the two young men and they left.

More hate came to town when a swastika-covered rock was thrown through the church window. The townspeople called a meeting, which started a community group to stop the hate. Derek was at the meeting and gave his opinion on why it would be best for the town to not start the group. Oh yes, he was very convincing. So nothing got done. How sad. But Tess, one of the angels, told Matt to tell exactly what he saw that night. Finally, he opened up and told the truth. He saw the two men beat up the assistant, but he also saw someone in the back seat of the car. They were just watching, looking on and saying nothing. When this person turned around, it was Satan, who had taken over Derek's body. His eyes were pure evil. There was no love at all.

> So humble yourselves before God. Resist the devil, and he will flee from you. (James 4:7NLT)

> Be sober, be vigilant; because your adversary the devil, as a roaring lion, walketh about, seeking whom he may devour. (1 Peter 5:8 KJV)

We know how sneaky Satan is. Oh yes, he is a trickster, always around trying to cause trouble and division. And that's exactly what he did in this episode of the show. He caused division with the people in town. He tried to bring on racism, hate, anger, selfishness, fear—everything you can think of that is evil. But the scripture says to resist the devil, and he will flee (James 4:7). Praise God, that is what the people did.

Everyone in town gathered to confront Derek and the two young men. Matt talked about love, and how he knew that God loved him. He talked about what God called him to be, a baker. So he baked bread for the town, and they shared the bread. Praise God, the bread of life—Jesus.

There was nothing Satan/Derek could do. The townspeople resisted him, so he had to flee. And he did.

And with him went all the hate, all the anger, and all the racism. It was replaced with love.

See, my friend, when people come together in love—with the love of Jesus—the devil can't stand it. He has no choice but to flee.

If this fictional show can portray a story of love, why can't the church and God's people do the same? Don't ever say it's not easy, because it is easy. But yes, sometimes there are factors that keep God's people from loving each other and learning the truth.

In 3 John 9, we read a letter John wrote to the church about a leader named Diotrephes. Not much is known about Diotrephes, but there are several facts we do know. He was a leader of the church. He had refused a letter that John wrote to him. And he was a troublemaker. Remember them?

Oh yes, Diotrephes was something else. He caused all this havoc inside the church and distorted the truth about Jesus. Let's look at John 9:22: "His parents said this because they were afraid of the Jewish leaders, who had announced that anyone saying Jesus was the Messiah would be expelled from the synagogue" (John 9:22 NLT).

Here we are introduced to a young man who was born blind. Jesus had healed this man by putting mud over his eyes, and he did this on the Sabbath. Oh no! How dare Jesus heal someone on the Sabbath. What would the religious leaders think?

So the Pharisees (Jewish leaders) conducted an investigation. They had to get to the bottom of this. They questioned the parents of the young man to find out if he was their son. They had to know if he *really* was born blind. Of course, his parents didn't deny their son, but they could not answer how he was healed. His parents would not tell the leaders that Jesus had healed their son. Hence, this is why they wanted the leaders to ask him for themselves. If these parents had mentioned Jesus's name, they would have been kicked out or forced to leave the synagogue.

Think about this. A miracle had just occurred for this family. This young man was born blind and probably never thought he would ever be able to see. But the leaders of the church, instead of showing love to this family, did not want the name of Jesus spoken of. We know that Jesus is the truth (John 14:6). So in their minds, if the truth is not spoken, people can't grow and won't grow. It's all about control with any leader who purposely keeps the truth from being revealed.

This was the concern that John had about Diotrephes. This man was a leader in the church, and he loved being the leader. So he had commanding authority and influence (*Merriam-Webster's Dictionary*), the definition of a leader.

Look at 3 John 9. Let's read exactly what type of person he was.

> Earlier I wrote something along the lines to the church, but Diotrephes, who loves being in charge, denigrates my counsel. (3 John 9 MSG)

> I wrote unto the church; but Diotrephes, who loveth to have the preeminence among them, receiveth us not. (3 John 9 KJV)

Let's take a closer look here. Diotrephes rejected John's spiritual covering. Remember John learned how to love by being one of Christ's disciples. And, therefore, he was able to take others, like Gaius, under his wing. But Diotrephes rejected or denigrated John's counsel. Basically, what he did was reject the teachings of Christ and create his own doctrine. The Bible doesn't state how he became a leader. It doesn't share his background or his gifts.

A few questions should be asked. How did Diotrephes become a leader in the church? Who appointed him?

Choose Wisely

Making simple choices can leave us feeling frustrated and unsure. Every day we have to make a choice, for example, go to work or take a sick day. Pay the light bill or buy groceries. If we make the wrong choice, it could have serious consequences.

A similar concept has plagued the church for years. Not every leader of the church should have been appointed leader in the first place. Let's take a look at 1 Timothy.

Paul wrote 1 Timothy to give encouragement and instruction for the young leader, Timothy. Paul was Timothy's spiritual father, so he had the obligation to train him. And he did just that.

> This is a trustworthy saying, "If someone aspires to be a church leader, he desires an honorable position. So a church leader must be a man whose life is above reproach. He must be faithful to his wife. He must exercise self-control, live wisely, and have a good reputation. He must enjoy

having guests in his home, and he must
be able to teach. He must not be a heavy
drinker or be violent. He must be gentle,
not quarrelsome, and not love money. He
must manage his own family well, having
children who respect and obey him. For if
a man cannot manage his own household,
how can he take care of God's church? (1
Timothy 3:1–5 NLT)

That was quite a list, but it was necessary. A leader
must be able to show love to people from all walks of life.
Would you want to have a leader who was violent or who
cheated on his or her spouse? I know I wouldn't. And this
type of behavior could cause others to follow. They might
say, "If my leader can do it, why can't I?" God knows that
is a dangerous path.

Not everyone who's a member of a church or even just
attends is strong in his or her faith. Each of us have our
own level of faith. Something that might just roll off your
shoulders could be detrimental to another.

Diotrephes was a dangerous leader. He was not only
making false accusations against believers, he refused to
show love to the traveling teachers. But the sad part was that
he told others in the church not to show love. My God from
Zion. How in the world was he ever chosen?

Never be in a hurry about appointing a
church leader. Do not share in the sins of
others. Keep yourself pure. (1 Timothy
5:22 NLT)

> Lay hands suddenly on no man, neither be
> partaker of other men's sins: keep thyself
> pure. (1 Timothy 5:22 KJV)

What exactly is this scripture saying? Well, for starters, Paul was instructing Timothy not to be in such a rush to appoint a leader. If he and others did put someone in a leadership role with unconfessed sin, it would make them accomplices. Oh yes. To be a partaker means to take part of something or share an experience. To participate. Ouch. Those are some harsh words, but they are true. Just knowing of sin and doing nothing about it is just as bad as the act itself.

I love watching crime shows. I can't get enough of them. They are full of real-life stories about people who committed some of the most heinous crimes imaginable. Sometimes there are two or more people involved in the crime, but only one commits the actual crime. The ones who are the lookouts or the getaway drivers are known as accomplices. They are associated or partakers with the crime.

When the cops arrest the suspect and bring him or her in for interrogation, they usually ask, "Who is your accomplice?" Meaning, who knows about this wrongdoing? The suspect may not give a name, but sometimes he or she does. I would; I'm not going down with the ship. Once the accomplice is identified, there is a trial, and those involved are convicted or freed. What blows my mind is that I have seen the accomplice get a longer prison sentence than the one who actually did the crime. Can you believe that? Knowing that something is wrong makes you and me just as guilty.

What Paul was implying was that believers in the body of Christ are just as responsible as the leaders for the growth and guidance of new believers. If an appointed leader is not showing love to others, we are held accountable. Ignoring the sin results in complacency. As sure as you're born, someone will say, "They are judging me." Calling out sin for what it is has nothing to do with judgment. That statement has plagued the church for many years. Many in the body of Christ are so afraid to speak up about the sins of leaders.

Judgment means to form an opinion, a divine sentence, or decision (*Merriam-Webster's Dictionary*). If I go around saying that all sinners are going to hell, I have formed an opinion based on my beliefs. That is judging. I have no right to say where a person's soul will end up because I am not God. But we do have the right to say that sin is wrong, and we will not promote it. We do have the right to say this person's or leader's lifestyle and choices are not acceptable in God's church. But keep in mind we have to make sure our own lives are acceptable to God. Don't just go around calling out others for their sins while ignoring yours.

Think about this. Diotrephes was placed in the position as a leader. I think we can say that John did not appoint Diotrephes as the leader. Maybe he trusted the local church to appoint a great leader. Obviously this did not happen. He rejected everything that John tried to teach the other leaders. He spread lies and distorted the love of Christ. Look at 3 John 10: "Not only does he refuse to welcome the traveling teachers, he also tells others not to help them. And when they do help, he puts them out of the church."

You might think, *You have got to be kidding me!* I'm afraid not, my friend. Stuff like this has been happening since the beginning. This man would not only refuse to help or show love to others but he told the people of the church to hate as well. And when they ignored his lies and showed love, he put them out of the church.

Remember what the Pharisees did to the parents of the blind man? They would not allow him to talk about Jesus. I can't even imagine. How could a leader in God's house knowingly tell the people not to show any love to strangers or each other?

I'm pretty sure you have heard the saying, "This is why I don't go to church." Maybe you have said it. But what is the "why" that would keep a person from church? In one sense it could be the lack of love that a leader shows. That would be the logical answer. But on the other hand, it is most likely something else.

Look at 3 John 11: "Dear friend, don't let this bad example influence you. Follow only what is good. Remember that those who do good prove that they are God's children, and those who do evil prove that they do not know God."

John continues with his letter to the church. At this point, he got word that some people were leaving the church by their own will because of Diotrephes. They probably vowed never to come back to the church because of all the hate this man displayed. But look at what John wrote: "Don't let this bad example influence you."

According to *Merriam-Webster's Dictionary,* the word *influence* means the power or capacity of causing an effect in indirect or intangible ways, to sway. The word *effect* means the power to bring about a result, to influence.

We see how Diotrephes loves to do things his own way. We see that he distorts the truth and lies about people to satisfy his own desires. So if he is going around twisting the truth and the love of Christ, he is entertaining sin. Now look at the definitions of *influence* and *effect.* They both begin with the word *power.* If someone has power over you, that individual has control over you.

Be very careful about what you see or hear. If Diotrephes could teach his followers not to love, he could teach them anything that was contrary to the Word of God. If you are in a church or ministry that teaches the opposite of the Word of God, you need to leave immediately. Run if you have to.

Diotrephes was an evil man. Sad to say, but it's true. He rejected John's authority, he rejected the love of Christ, he rejected the truth, he caused division in the church, he excommunicated churchgoers for not agreeing with him, he was self-seeking, and he was self-righteous. He was *not* a man of God. I think it's fair to say that he didn't know God at all. For the scripture says, "And those who do evil prove that they do not know God." His actions, character, and his words gave him away. We must always be careful not to follow or listen to such a person. My friends, Diotrephes might not have agreed with what John was saying. He may have felt that he could do a better job as leader. So instead of embracing John's teaching on the love of Christ, he developed hatred. He flat out wanted the church to feel the same way as him. But look at the last scripture in this text.

> Everyone speaks highly of Demetrius, as does the truth itself. We ourselves can say the same for him, and you know we speak the truth. (3 John 12 NLT)

> Demetrius has a good testimony from all,
> and from the truth itself. And we also bear
> witness, and you know that our testimony
> is true. (3 John 12 NKJV)

Demetrius is a breath of fresh air. He seems like a really nice Christian man. But let's go a little deeper. We just read a few verses ago about an ungodly man named Diotrephes. We learned that nothing good came from his leadership. He had no love for people and rebuked those who did love.

And here we have Demetrius. Though we do not know much about him, we know that people speak highly of him. People notice the man he is. They notice his character, attitude, and most importantly, the truth.

Read 1 Kings 17:24:

> Then the woman told Elijah, "Now I know
> for sure that you are a man of God, and
> that the Lord truly speaks through you." (1
> Kings 17:24 NLT)

> And the woman said to Elijah, "Now by
> this I know that thou are a man of God,
> and that the word of the Lord in thy mouth
> is truth. (1 Kings 17:24 KJV)

"Okay, Tamera, what do Demetrius and Elijah have in common?" I am so glad you asked.

In 1 Kings 17, we learned of the widow and her son. God instructed Elijah to go to the village of Zarephath and meet this woman. God was using the woman to feed Elijah, but she did not know God for herself: "But she said, 'I swear by the Lord your God that I don't have a single piece of bread in the house. And I have only a handful of flour left in the jar and a little cooking oil in the bottom of the jug. I was just gathering a few sticks to cook this last mean, and then my son and I will die'" (1 Kings 17:12 NLT).

She told Elijah, "the Lord your God." She knew of God but had never experienced him for herself.

And what did Elijah say next? "But Elijah said to her, 'Don't be afraid! Go ahead and do just what you've said, but make a little bread for me first. Then use what's left to prepare a meal for yourself and your son'" (1 Kings 17:13 NLT).

Now hold on a minute. I can imagine what this woman was thinking: *Did this man, whom I don't know, just ask me to give him something to eat first before my son and I eat? Did he not just hear me say that I had only enough for us? Was he not listening? Is this God? Surely the God of Israel is not like this? Why would I want to follow a God like this who knows that we have no food?* We have no idea what she was truly thinking or feeling. I know some of us would not have been too kind. You can be honest. Praise God.

And then he keeps on talking:

> For this is what the Lord, the God of Israel says: "There will always be flour and olive oil left in your containers until the time when the Lord sends rain and the crops grow again." (1 Kings 17:14 NLT)

> For thus saith the Lord God of Israel, The barrel of meal shall not waste, neither shall

> the cruse (a small vessel or jar) of oil fail,
> until the day that the Lord sendeth rain
> upon the earth. (1 Kings 17:14 KJV)

So the woman did what Elijah told her to do. When he spoke the truth, he spoke for God. She heard it; she saw it. But then the unthinkable happened. Her son died. Now she was back to square one.

God spoke his truth through Elijah by supplying plenty of flour and oil for her household. But now her son was dead. She must have thought, *Why is this happening? Father God, what are you doing?* She was angry with Elijah, thinking he had come to punish her for her sins (1 Kings 17:18).

But Elijah knew who his God was. He knew his God was a miracle worker. He knew his God was truth. So he asked God to return life unto the boy. And he did!

Once again, this woman, this mother, saw the power of God. She saw that this man whom she didn't know was speaking God's truth, speaking God's love. God loved both Elijah and this woman just as he loves us today. But she may not have felt God's love in the same way. She may have felt that God loved everyone except her. Have you ever heard people say that? I know I have. Through Elijah, this woman learned the truth that God is love and that Elijah came with a blessing for her household.

The same truth that Elijah walked in was the same truth that Demetrius walked in. Go back to 3 John, where we see that everyone spoke highly of Demetrius. It is unclear whether Demetrius was a prophet, but one thing was for sure: he was a man of God. He spoke God's truth, and he spoke in love. People not only heard about it, but they saw it with their own eyes. Demetrius was the complete opposite of Diotrephes. He didn't go around keeping people down or depriving people of God. No, he spoke God's truth.

Think about this, my friend. If you and I are interested in going to a vacation destination or eating at a fancy restaurant, the first thing we take into account are word-of-mouth recommendations. When someone speaks highly of something, we take that into consideration. We base whether we go on this vacation or the restaurant on experience.

Can you imagine what the widow told others about Elijah's God? What the people in the church said about Jesus? After they were hurt by Diotrephes, Demetrius showed them love. So the next time someone says, "This is why I stopped going to church," love on them. Show them God's love. They may have just experienced a Diotrephes. You can be that Demetrius. You can speak truth. You can speak love. You can speak Jesus. Amen.

All It Takes Is Love, Not Lip Service

Dear friend, love is such a powerful tool. It takes so much more than just saying the words; it's showing the actions. We learned that love is a gift. And when we give gifts, we don't take them back. The world today is filled with much turmoil and heartache. We have the power to love the hell out of that hate. To love the hell out of that man, that woman. To love the hell out of our governments, our communities. Yes, we have that power.

Jesus loved his disciples. He loved the people, the Gentiles. He loved his mother, and she became a covering over John. My friend, love on people. But always remember to love yourself first. Once you do that, loving on people will come naturally. It won't always be easy. God knows it won't. But it is necessary. It's about God's kingdom. It's about Jesus. It's about that soul.

Earlier you wrote down the names of people who are hard to love. Next to it, you put what was hard to love about them. Take that paper and tear it down the middle. Throw away the piece with all the negative traits. Now you are left with just their names. Look at those names. Embrace them because this is what God sees. This is what he remembers.

Gospel recording artist Tasha Cobbs has a song titled "You Know My Name." God loves us when we are difficult, when we are moody. He knows our names. My friend, know the names. Think about how you would feel if someone called you out of your name. You know what I'm getting at. We would be hurt, upset, and mad. Yes, and that too!

Jesus gave his life because he loved us. He still does. He gave it knowing everyone would not love him back. That is power. Do not look for perfection out of people. You will be disappointed. Know there are flaws and mishaps, but love anyway. Don't run from God. No, the church is not perfect. The leaders are not perfect, and yes, some are downright evil. But love anyway. Speak God's truth. Speak God's love language. Open your heart. You never know who may come into your path.

Everywhere we look there is hate. We may not agree with the lifestyles of others, their political parties, or their churches. But we can love them. Love the hell out of them. Loving on them doesn't mean you agree with their choices. God doesn't agree with our choices, and sometimes we make bad ones. But he knows our names.

My friend, I love you. I pray for you. Pray for me. Keep on loving. Let's love the hell out of people together. Jesus loves the hell out of us. And some of us have more hell in us than we know.

God bless you, friend.

Father, I love you this day. Forgive me for not loving on the ones that I thought were difficult to love. Forgive me for not loving on them like you love on me for I do not wrestle against flesh and blood but against principalities. I walk in your love language. My heart is open to love. Father, I love the hell out of people, out of my community, and out of this nation. Father, I love the hell out of this government and our elected officials. I will not worry whether they are right or wrong for you will handle that in due time. I just love on them today. You are so worthy, and I thank you for your love. In Jesus's name. Amen.

Love Language

Read these scriptures aloud on a daily basis. Add names if you have to. Believe God. Trust in him.

> Above all, keep loving one another earnestly, since love covers a multitude of sins. (1 Peter 4:8 NLT)

Above all, I will keep loving [add a name] earnestly, since love covers a multitude of sins.

> Anyone who does not love does not know God, because God is love. (1 John 4:8 NLT)

Anyone who does not love [name government official] does not know God because God is love.

Let love be genuine. Abhor what is evil; hold
fast to what is good. (Romans 12:9 NLT)

Prophetic Page

I know that we just read about love and learned about love. Writing this book was a humbling experience. Never did I think I could or would write a book. I know what God gave me years ago, but I ran away from it. During many times of great sorrow and pain, God was never away from me. He did feel far from me, but he wasn't. I have seen so much going on in this world, and it breaks my heart. God has given me so much. And I knew that I walked in the prophetic. But like so much, I ran from my calling. My friend, just know this: God has given me this to say. I can only relay what has been said unto me.

My beloved, I hear people say all the time that love is love. And yes, love is love. But Satan has twisted the way I created people to love because he is not love. I created this earth because I love you. I knew your name before you were born. I knew you would go through life with questions, confusion. I knew that people would hate you, and you would hate people. I knew all those things. I hear the cries; I hear the prayers. I hear it all.

I see the hatred for my children who are not living the lives I want for them. Yes, I know those who are homosexual, those who are married, those who are fornicating, and those who are adulterers. I know those who have committed murder, those who have stolen, and those who aborted their children.

I know them all, and I see them all. I watch what they do in the morning. And I watch what they do at night. Yes, I see it all. No, I am not pleased with everything they do. But I love them.

I created man. I saw that man had no one for himself. So I created woman. I created a "her" for a "him." Satan has twisted it all around. Yes, love is love. But do you not know that I created sex as well. Oh yes, I Am created sex. I created a man to have sex with a woman. A husband to have sex with his wife. I see you men who are having sex with other men. I see you female pastors who are having sex with other women. I see you male pastors who stand before my people and preach, and then go home at night and have sex with another man. Oh yes, I see all that. But I love you.

You keep saying, "God is love." And yes, I am love. I am the Alpha and Omega. But how can I create sex for a man and a woman and then accept sex between two men or two women? How can I accept this? I am not pleased with it. But I still love you.

I created you, the man, and you, the woman, to produce a life. I am the Creator of life. I give life. I breathe life. But how can life come from two of the same things? If you bake a cake, you will need different ingredients. How can you bake a cake with just two eggs?

Homosexuality is detestable because I want my people clean. Not because I don't love but because I will not go back on what I created sex for. Love is love, but homosexuality is not based on love. It is lust for the flesh. I knew this would happen. But I still love.

There is nothing wrong with two men loving each other nor two women loving each other. That is great. This is philia or phileo love (Romans 12:10): love that is shown by friendship or affection. To love as a brother or sister. But when you add sex to this, it is no longer based on love. This is where your flesh takes over.

You just read about Gaius and Demetrius. They walked in love and my truth. They did not twist my truth to please themselves or others. I was pleased with them because they walked in love. Beloved, just know this. I Am is a jealous God. Read Exodus 34:14. Oh yes, I said it. I don't want to share you with other gods. No, I am not talking only about statues. I am talking about anything that gets in the way of our relationship. I want your mind; I want your spirit. And yes, I want your body. For your body is a temple (1 Corinthians 6:19–20).

My Word will not change. I loved you before you were born. I love you on your good days and bad days. I love you when you get it right and when you make mistakes. I love you.

Yes, I see those people who claim to love in my name. I see their hate. When they hurt you, they hurt me. I see the church. I know what they are doing. No, I am not pleased with everything. I will deal with that in due time. But I want you back. Some of you have never given me a chance. You have treated me the way people have treated you. With hatred. I have always been there. I was never far away. I loved you then, and I love you now.

Not all people are like the ones you have met or seen before. No, God does not hate those who walk in homosexuality. But I am not pleased. Those that walk in truth represent my kingdom. I don't like religion either. The religious have lied about me for too long. I do not hate you. But My Word will not return to me void. You can continue to walk in homosexuality, pleasing your flesh and calling it love. But soon, very soon, every knee will bow, and every tongue will confess unto me (Romans 14:11).

Yes, I am watching you. I see everything you do. And you pastors, preachers of the gospel who tell the people that I hate them, shame on you unless you repent, and then I will deal with you. To you pastors who walk in the spirit of homosexuality, shame on you unless you repent, and then I will deal with you. Yes I see sin. No sin is worse than the other for sin is sin.

I saw the mother who aborted her child, my gift to her. Yes, I saw it. Did you show her love? Did you hate on her? When she repents, I will do a greater work through her. Love on her. Embrace her. You have no idea how she feels. I do. I know her pain. I love her.

I saw all those school shootings, how the murderer deliberately took lives away. Yes, I saw it. I was not pleased. Their sin is not greater or lesser than others. But I love them. With a repented heart, I will do great things through them.

You are thinking, *God, how can you see it all and let it all happen? If you are so good, like those Christians say, why do you let bad things happen?*

My child, my Son told you that there would be "great tribulation in this world" (John 16:33). You will not understand it all, but know it is all for a purpose. I want more of you to become intercessors, to become missionaries. To become spiritual fathers and mothers. I want more love from you and through you. People need to see me through you. I love you. I know what is happening in this world. I see how my children are being treated in those prisons in Texas. You call them detention centers; I call them prisons. I hear their cries. I am about to rescue them. I am about to bless them. I am doing a new thing in them already. I, the Lord, have spoken.

To my sons and daughters, please know that I do love you. There is so much I want to do through you. There is so much I want to say through you. But I will not go back on my Word. I have spoken through my prophet. Seek me while I may be found (Isaiah 55:6–7).

Walk in love for this pleases me. Pray for your leaders. I see what they do. I hear what they are doing. I am not pleased with everything. But I still love. I love them, and I love you.

My child, walk in love. This is my commandment. I want your attention. I want to do many great things through you. Walk in love for I love you, my child.

References

New Living Translation Bible. Tyndale House Publishing, 2019.

The King James Version Study Bible. Barbour Publishing, 2011.

The Message: The Bible in Contemporary Language. Eugene H. Peterson, 2005.

Printed in the United States
By Bookmasters